I am Gandhi

BRAD MELTZER

illustrated by Christopher Eliopoulos

 DIAL BOOKS FOR YOUNG READERS

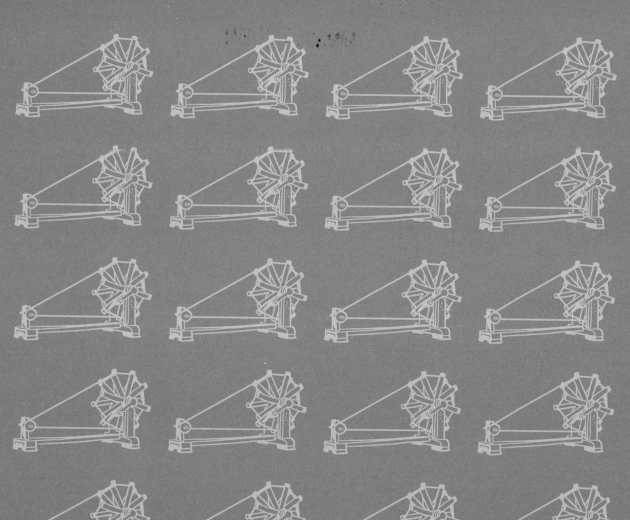

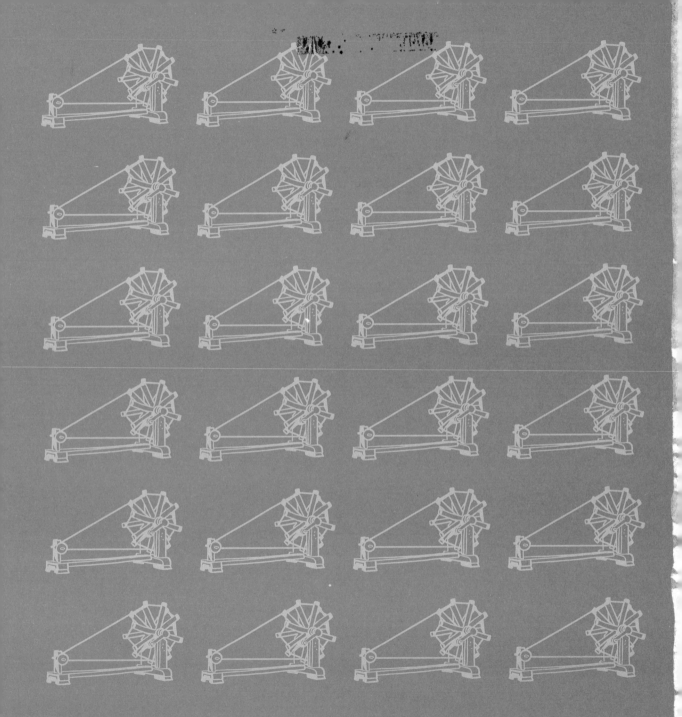

I am Gandhi.

Today, people call me strong.
Unafraid.
Unstoppable.
I wasn't always that way.
As a child growing up in India,
I was shy.
Afraid of the dark.
I was also afraid of snakes.

Can you tell I was small?
I spent most of my time
with books.

OOH, A SNAKE—WANT TO SEE IT?

I WOULD VERY MUCH **NOT** LIKE TO SEE IT.

I wasn't good at sports, like soccer.

In fact, I'd run home after school, afraid that people would make fun of me.

But I liked taking nice long walks.

Even with all my books, I wasn't a great student.
I was bad at multiplication.
And one day, when I got one of our spelling words wrong,
the teacher pointed to another boy's paper.

I didn't think that was the right thing to do.
That's not how you learn.
When the teacher scolded me, I wasn't bothered.
In my life, I did not copy others' work.

However, there was one story that was worth copying.
It was a play I read in school about a man named Shravan Kumar.
Shravan was so devoted to his parents that when they were too
old to travel, he literally carried them on his back.

It was an example I wanted to follow.
One person carrying others who needed help.

My father had a good job.
He was a political leader.
But there were many who had no jobs.
They were the poorest of the poor.
They were treated terribly and had the worst jobs.
There were even different laws that applied to them.

MOHANDAS, SEE HOW MANY POOR THERE ARE?

WHEN YOU ARE BORN POOR, LIFE IS HARD ENOUGH.

BUT IN INDIA, THERE WAS A GROUP OF PEOPLE CALLED THE "UNTOUCHABLES,"

WHO WEREN'T ALLOWED TO MAKE A BETTER LIFE FOR THEMSELVES.

Back then, the British were so powerful, they ruled India. To get a good job like my father, I eventually moved to London, England, and became a lawyer.
I even dressed up real fancy, trying to look rich and more British.

When I moved back to India, I had my first case in court.
This was the moment I trained for.
All I had to do was question the witness.

The moment I stood up, my heart sank to my boots.
It was like the room was spinning.

I sat back down without a word.

That was my first case.
I completely failed.

Luckily, I got offered a new case in a country called South Africa. I was excited to try again.

As I took the last part of my journey by train, a white passenger noticed me...

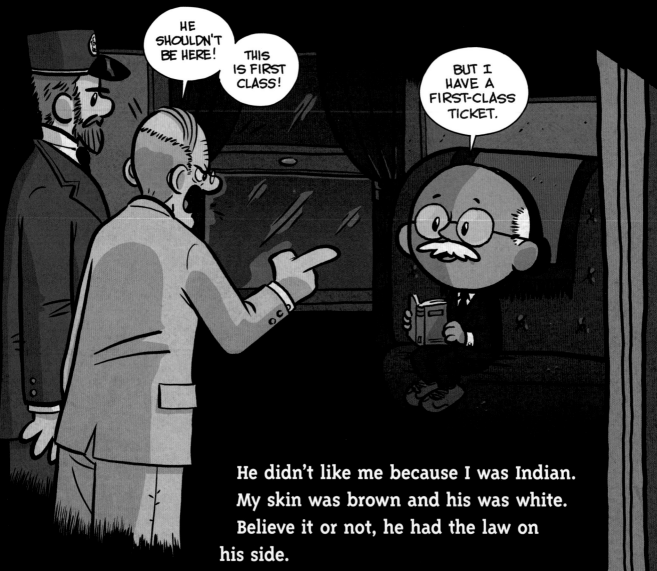

HE SHOULDN'T BE HERE!

THIS IS FIRST CLASS!

BUT I HAVE A FIRST-CLASS TICKET.

He didn't like me because I was Indian. My skin was brown and his was white. Believe it or not, he had the law on his side.

The train official asked me to leave.

He said that if I didn't leave, he'd call the police.

"Yes, you may," I told him. "I refuse to get out voluntarily."

WHY DON'T YOU GO SIT IN THIRD CLASS WHERE YOU BELONG?

A policeman pushed me out of the train and tossed my stuff onto the station platform.

It was cold in that station. And dark. I could've gotten back on the train and sat in third class.

Instead, I stayed there all night. Shivering.

I also meditated, which is when you close your eyes and try to focus your mind.

To finish the trip, I took a horse-drawn carriage.

But once again, because of my skin color, they didn't let me sit inside with the white passengers.

The driver hit me in the ears and tried to drag me down. I never hit him back. But I refused to let go.

Eventually, he gave up.
But this is how Indians were treated back then.
To change it, I knew I had to take action. I had to fight.
Even if it meant suffering hardship.

Within a week, I held a meeting for my fellow Indians in South Africa.
It was the first public speech of my life.
I focused on the truth.

After the speech, we all had a discussion.
There are times to talk.
But there is also real power in listening.

Soon after, I decided to stay in South Africa and formed the Natal Indian Congress to help Indians there become more active in the government.

But the most important thing I did there was come up with *Satyagraha*.

SAY IT WITH ME: SUHT-YAH-GRUH-HUH.

In Sanskrit, it combines the word *satya*, which means "truth," with *agraha*, which means "firmness" or "force."

TRUTH FORCE?

IT SOUNDS LIKE A SUPERHERO TEAM!

TRUTH FORCE!

Indeed. Satyagraha was my Truth Force. Satyagraha was how we'd fight against the unfair treatment of Indians.

1) NONCOOPERATION OR CIVIL DISOBEDIENCE: PROTESTING AN UNFAIR LAW IN A NONVIOLENT WAY

2) NONVIOLENCE = USING LOVE AND PEACEFUL METHODS

3) NONPOSSESSION = LIVING A SIMPLE LIFE THAT USES ONLY WHAT YOU NEED, NOTHING MORE

IS THAT WHY HE DRESSED IN JUST A SIMPLE CLOTH?

THAT'S THE REASON.

TRUTH FORCE!

Was I perfect? No.
Sometimes I lost my temper.
But that's when I figured out the best way to fight,
by transforming myself and being the best person I could be.

In no time at all, I tested out Satyagraha.

A new law was passed that would kick Indians out of South Africa unless they registered with the government.

Police could stop us on the street and search our homes any time they wanted.

For breaking that law, they put me in prison for two months. They put me there again for breaking another law, one that said Indians couldn't travel to certain areas.

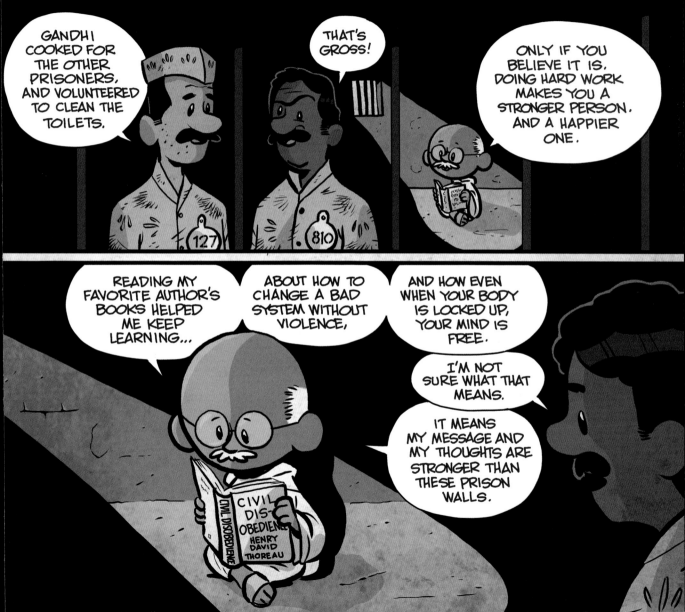

You know what's even stronger than that?
People working together.
Soon, we started more settlements and farms where those
who practiced Satyagraha could live a simple life in peace.

As our "peace army" grew, so did our strength.

When the South African government made Indians pay more taxes than white residents and refused to improve the safety of coal miners, we decided to protest by striking.

It was just like Thoreau taught.

Instead of using violence to protest the unfair rules, Indian people used a peaceful method: No one went to work at the coal mines.

Without workers, the coal companies would go out of business.

Now the only question was: Would it succeed?

It took years, but the South Africa government passed the Indian Relief Act of 1914, improving the lives of many Indians.

After twenty-one years, it was time to take what I had learned in South Africa...

back to my home in India.

India was still being run by the British, who treated us terribly.

And worst of all, Indians still treated some other Indians terribly too.

To protest the unfair British laws in India, we held another strike.
For one full day, no one went to work.
All of India—every shop, farm, restaurant—closed down.

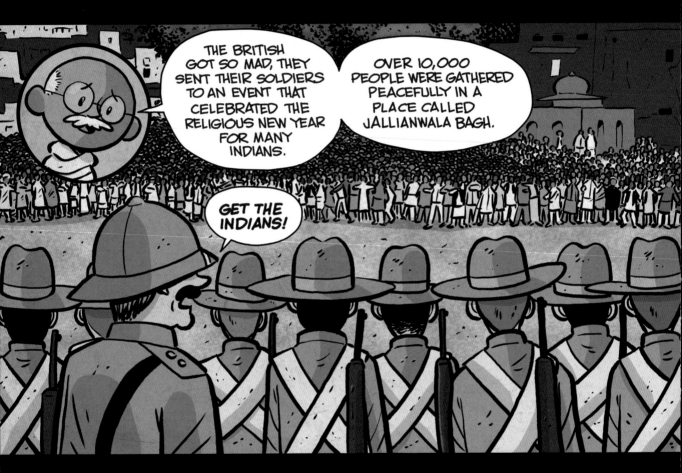

THE BRITISH GOT SO MAD, THEY SENT THEIR SOLDIERS TO AN EVENT THAT CELEBRATED THE RELIGIOUS NEW YEAR FOR MANY INDIANS.

OVER 10,000 PEOPLE WERE GATHERED PEACEFULLY IN A PLACE CALLED JALLIANWALA BAGH.

GET THE INDIANS!

The soldiers attacked the crowd.
Over a thousand were injured. Hundreds were killed.
They hit us. Hard.
It was tempting to hit them back.

But violence will never get you what you want.
As the head of our own organization, the Indian National Congress...

I KNOW WHAT WE MUST DO.

TRUTH FORCE!

PLEASE SAY WE'RE USING TRUTH FORCE AGAIN!

We did.

INSTEAD OF BUYING BRITISH CLOTHING, I URGED PEOPLE TO USE SPINNING WHEELS LIKE THIS TO MAKE THEIR OWN CLOTHES.

I WOULD SPIN THREAD EVERY DAY. I EVEN MADE THIS COOL OUTFIT.

BY REPRESENTING INDEPENDENCE, HIS SPINNING WHEEL BECAME SO POPULAR, IT WAS ON THE ORIGINAL DESIGN FOR INDIA'S FLAG.

I called for massive boycotts, which meant we would stop going to British schools and stop working for British employers.

I had to make sure that as many people as possible heard my message. To do that, I relied on the same thing as when I was younger. I walked.

INDIA WAS OVER A MILLION SQUARE MILES.

THE POOR LIVED IN HARD-TO-REACH VILLAGES, SO I TRAVELLED TO THEM.

FOR SEVEN MONTHS, I ATE THE SAME MEAL THREE TIMES A DAY:

SIXTEEN OUNCES OF GOAT'S MILK,

THREE SLICES OF TOAST,

TWO ORANGES,

AND SOME GRAPES OR RAISINS.

Only by standing together—rich and poor—could we be free from this unfair government.

Only united are we unstoppable.

That didn't mean everyone was on my side.

Even though my work against the government was peaceful, the British again put me in prison—this time for six years.

I smiled as they took me to jail.

I DID NOT MIND PRISON.

IT ALLOWED ME TIME TO READ, PRAY, LEARN...

AND KEEP SPINNING.

But within two years, I got sick there.

The government knew people would be enraged if something happened to me, so they let me out.

I went right back to my mission. The British government still wouldn't leave India.

They passed new laws called the Salt Acts, which said Indians couldn't make or sell our own salt.

We had to buy it from the British.

How could we convince the British?

We marched.

On March 12, 1930, seventy-eight people joined me as we headed toward the sea.

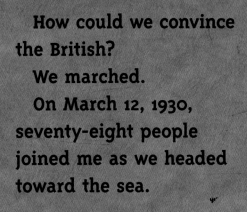

I was sixty years old, walking 240 miles.
Ten miles each day for nearly a month.

The farther we walked, the more people joined us.
They poured water on our paths, to keep the dust down.
They tossed flowers and leaves to make it easier to walk on.

The crowd soon ballooned to thousands, stretching back for two miles.
Reporters around the world told our story.

Twenty-four days later, we reached our destination: the village of Dandi, near the Arabian Sea.

There, I gave my signal to the nation.

WHAT'S HE DOING?

THERE'S SOMETHING IN THE SAND!

I picked up a handful of salt left by the waves.

That's it.

I never raised my fists.

I never carried a weapon.

But in that act—holding salt that wasn't bought from the British government—I fought back. I broke the law.

With the entire world watching.

Soon after, I was arrested. Again.

But over the next few days, thousands of Indians broke the same law.

Just a few clumps of salt united our people and made the whole world realize how poorly the British were treating us.

From there, it still took years, but we were on our way to India becoming a free country.

My struggles weren't done, though. Remember the untouchables—the poorest of the poor? They were still suffering.

I was in jail, but I could act.

They could lock me up. They could put me in the dark.
But they could never, ever defeat me.

In my life,
I was the small one.
The skinny one.
The poor one.
Even the shy one.
But I was never the weak one.

Over many years, I had many fights.
But to fight by purposely avoiding violence?
To refuse to raise your fist, no matter what is raised against you?
Some would call that foolish.
Madness.
But what it really is...

TRUTH FORCE!

is courage.

TODAY, GANDHI'S FAMOUS SATYAGRAHA IS AS POWERFUL AS EVER.
IT INSPIRED CIVIL RIGHTS MOVEMENTS ALL ACROSS THE WORLD, INCLUDING THOSE LED BY MARTIN LUTHER KING JR. AND NELSON MANDELA.

Strength doesn't come from the size of your body.
It comes from the size of your heart.
Show love, especially when you want to fight unfairness.

You must help others who are in need.
Carry them on your shoulders.
Speak up for them when they don't have a voice.
Hold true to your beliefs.

TRUTH FORCE!

I am Gandhi,
and in a gentle way,
I will shake the world.

"In a gentle way, you can shake the world."
—Gandhi

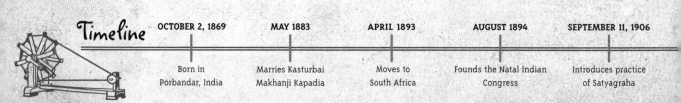

Timeline

OCTOBER 2, 1869

Born in
Porbandar, India

MAY 1883

Marries Kasturbai
Makhanji Kapadia

APRIL 1893

Moves to
South Africa

AUGUST 1894

Founds the Natal Indian
Congress

SEPTEMBER 11, 1906

Introduces practice
of Satyagraha

Gandhi at
age seven

Gandhi at his
spinning wheel

The Salt
March

The current
Indian flag

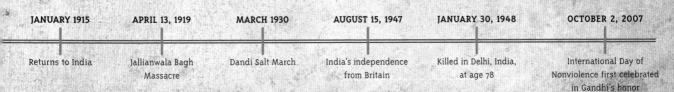

JANUARY 1915	APRIL 13, 1919	MARCH 1930	AUGUST 15, 1947	JANUARY 30, 1948	OCTOBER 2, 2007
Returns to India	Jallianwala Bagh Massacre	Dandi Salt March	India's independence from Britain	Killed in Delhi, India, at age 78	International Day of Nonviolence first celebrated in Gandhi's honor

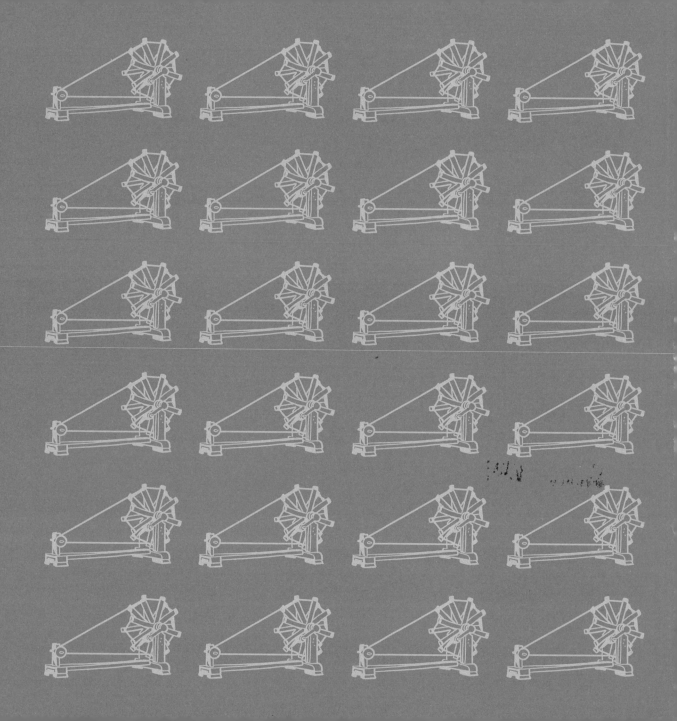